The Good Thief

The Good Thief

M A R I E   H O W E

The National Poetry Series
Selected by Margaret Atwood

A Karen and Michael Braziller Book
PERSEA BOOKS / NEW YORK

ACKNOWLEDGMENTS

I wish to thank the following magazines for publishing some of the poems that appear in this book: *The Atlantic, The American Poetry Review, Poetry, Ploughshares, The Agni Review, The Partisan Review,* and *Shankpainter.* "Death, the last visit" and "Menses" also appeared in *A Celebration for Stanley Kunitz,* published by The Sheep Meadow Press.

I am grateful to The Fine Arts Work Center in Provincetown, The St. Botolph Foundation, The Massachusetts Artists Foundation, and The MacDowell Colony for their aid and support; to Charlot and Peter Davenport for the meadow; and to many dear friends, too many to mention here, for their sustaining encouragement during the writing of this book. But I need to particularly thank Askold Melnyczuk, Stuart Dischell, Steven Cramer, Jorie Graham, Lucie Brock-Broido, Nancy Crumbine, and Tom Sleigh for their specific and patient criticism of these poems. Finally, I am forever grateful to my brother, John Howe, and my teacher, Stanley Kunitz.

M. H.

For information, address the publisher:
Persea Books
171 Madison Avenue
New York, New York 10016

Library of Congress Cataloging-in-Publication Data

Howe, Marie, 1950-
   The good thief : poems / Marie Howe.
      p.   cm.—(National poetry series : 1987)
   ISBN: 0-89255-127-5 (pbk.) : $9.95
   I. Title.   II. Series.
PS3558.08925G6 1988
811'.54—dc19   88-4136   CIP

Designed by Peter St. John Ginna
Set in Electra by Keystrokes, Lenox, Massachusetts
Printed by Capital City Press, Montpelier, Vermont

Fifth Printing

For my father and mother,
and my sisters and brothers.

Contents

The Good Thief

The danger itself fosters the rescuing power
Hölderlin

Part of Eve's Discussion

It was like the moment when a bird decides not to eat from your hand,
and flies, just before it flies, the moment the rivers seem to still
and stop because a storm is coming, but there is no storm, as when
a hundred starlings lift and bank together before they wheel and drop,
very much like the moment, driving on bad ice, when it occurs to you
your car could spin, just before it slowly begins to spin, like
the moment just before you forgot what it was you were about to say,
it was like that, and after that, it was still like that, only
all the time.

Death, the last visit

Hearing a low growl in your throat, you'll know that it's started.
It has nothing to ask you. It has only something to say, and
it will speak in your own tongue.

Locking its arm around you, it will hold you as long as you ever wanted.
Only this time it will be long enough. It will not let go.
Burying your face in its dark shoulder, you'll smell mud and hair
       and water.

You'll taste your mother's sour nipple, your favorite salty cock
and swallow a word you thought you'd spit out once and be done with.
Through half-closed eyes you'll see that its shadow looks like yours,

a perfect fit. You could weep with gratefulness. It will take you
as you like it best, hard and fast as a slap across your face,
or so sweet and slow you'll scream give it to me give it to me until it does.

Nothing will ever reach this deep. Nothing will ever clench this hard.
At last (the little girls are clapping, shouting) someone has pulled
the drawstring of your gym bag closed enough and tight. At last

someone has knotted the lace of your shoe so it won't ever come undone.
Even as you turn into it, even as you begin to feel yourself stop,
you'll whistle with amazement between your residual teeth oh jesus

oh sweetheart, oh holy mother, nothing nothing nothing ever felt
       this good.

What the Angels Left

At first, the scissors seemed perfectly harmless.
They lay on the kitchen table in the blue light.

Then I began to notice them all over the house,
at night in the pantry, or filling up bowls in the cellar

where there should have been apples. They appeared under rugs,
lumpy places where one would usually settle before the fire,

or suddenly shining in the sink at the bottom of soupy water.
Once, I found a pair in the garden, stuck in turned dirt

among the new bulbs, and one night, under my pillow,
I felt something like a cool long tooth and pulled them out

to lie next to me in the dark. Soon after that I began
to collect them, filling boxes, old shopping bags,

every suitcase I owned. I grew slightly uncomfortable
when company came. What if someone noticed them

when looking for forks or replacing dried dishes? I longed
to throw them out, but how could I get rid of something

that felt oddly like grace? It occurred to me finally
that I was meant to use them, and I resisted a growing compulsion

to cut my hair, although, in moments of great distraction,
I thought it was my eyes they wanted, or my soft belly

—exhausted, in winter, I laid them out on the lawn.
The snow fell quite as usual, without any apparent hesitation

or discomfort. In spring, as I expected, they were gone.
In their place, a slight metallic smell, and the dear muddy earth.

The Mountain

It wasn't only the mountain then,
but the mountain later

rising in sleep
or deep in the middle of stuttered proclamation

when, startled, he saw it,
how it had looked to him before,

how it had felt underfoot
like the back of an animal

heaving him down over and over again,
and the small stones that fell with him

making a music
and the silence then.

Once, he put his ear to water almost weeping
to the mouth of a sleeping child

so many many dead.
And the gravelly walk down then

the stones singing
and the wrist of the branch that held him

when he caught it, held him up.
It wasn't only the mountain *then*, that day:

the sky clearing, his awful thirst,
but the day after,

and all the days when he, forever moving,
felt it move in him.

It was like that
but he could not say it.

It was what rose up in him one minute
before waking

what seemed to block his view whenever
he looked too closely at something

his son,
his own hand, his food sometimes.

Finally, can you understand how easily
he relinquished it? The grit

the cracked bone, the new land?
He was that tired of walking in what

he knew was the wrong direction.
And he knew

better than anyone, how long the way back was
to where he started,

when tending the lambs, day dreaming,
for no apparent reason, he looked up.

The Meadow

As we walk into words that have waited for us to enter them, so
the meadow, muddy with dreams, is gathering itself together

and trying, with difficulty, to remember how to make wildflowers.
Imperceptibly heaving with the old impatience, it knows

for certain that two horses walk upon it, weary of hay.
The horses, sway-backed and self-important, cannot design

how the small white pony mysteriously escapes the fence every day.
This is the miracle just beyond their heavy-headed grasp,

and they turn from his nuzzling with irritation. Everything
is crying out. Two crows, rising from the hill, fight

and caw-cry in mid-flight, then fall and light on the meadow grass
bewildered by their weight. A dozen wasps drone, tiny prop planes,

sputtering into a field the farmer has not yet plowed,
and what I thought was a phone, turned down and ringing,

is the knock of a woodpecker for food or warning, I can't say.
I want to add my cry to those who would speak for the sound alone.

But in this world, where something is always listening, even
murmuring has meaning, as in the next room you moan

in your sleep, turning into late morning. My love, this might be
all we know of forgiveness, this small time when you can forget

what you are. There will come a day when the meadow will think
suddenly, *water, root, blossom*, through no fault of its own,

and the horses will lie down in daisies and clover. Bedeviled,
human, your plight, in waking, is to choose from the words

that even now sleep on your tongue, and to know that tangled
among them and terribly new is the sentence that could change your life.

From Nowhere

I think the sea is a useless teacher, pitching and falling
no matter the weather, when our lives are rather lakes

unlocking in a constant and bewildering spring. Listen,
a day comes, when you say what all winter

I've been meaning to ask, and a crack booms and echoes
where ice had seemed solid, scattering ducks

and scaring us half to death. In Vermont, you dreamed
from the crown of a hill and across a ravine

you saw lights so familiar they might have been ours
shining back from the future.

And waking, you walked there, to the real place,
and when you saw only trees, came back bleak

with a foreknowledge we have both come to believe in.
But this morning, a kind day has descended, from nowhere,

and making coffee in the usual way, measuring grounds
with the wooden spoon, I remembered,

this is how things happen, cup by cup, familiar gesture
after gesture, what else can we know of safety

or of fruitfulness? We walk with mincing steps within
a thaw as slow as February, wading through currents

that surprise us with their sudden warmth. Remember,
last week you woke still whistling for a bird

that had miraculously escaped its cage, and look, today,
a swallow has come to settle behind this rented rain gutter,

gripping a twig twice his size in his beak, staggering
under its weight, so delicately, so precariously, it seems

from here, holding all he knows of hope in his mouth.

Bad Weather

What does it matter that this cold June breaks, another dish
on the kitchen floor, skittering under the table legs.
So it requires the long strawed broom, the extra stoop.
It will have out. When the sun comes back. When the rain stops.

But something doesn't fit. Something isn't fitting.
The washing machine jams and hums too loudly. The chickadees
fall from the trees. A swallow is caught in the chimney.
The smallest ram lamb isn't eating. The days pass.

June is too cold. The spiders threaten to overrun the nest
lodged in the rafters. They can't be eaten fast enough.
The mother, beside herself, has seen this happen only once before,
the eggs draped with gauze.

No letters come. The small tin flag is down. The house creeps
farther from the road. The grass rises in the rain. The scythes
rust and will not cut. The blades squeak and sigh, nothing
to be done. We close the porch doors, but every night

they open just a little. We hear it from the bedroom,
a small creak. no one there. The cold lies down in the meadow
where the sheep are credulous and sturdy and dumb, but
the ram lamb will not eat. His mother has already forgotten him.

The windows will not stay shut. Even the small nails
we bang in are loose in the morning, and the screens flap
a little in the small cold wind. From under the covers,
I watch you move around the house, fixing the broken things:

the desk lamp, the toaster, the radio that still will not speak.
The red hens haven't laid in a week. There's nothing we can do.
Nothing. It could be ten years ago. I could be dreaming.
This could be last winter all over again

with the wood stacked and the snow rushing from miles away. Then too, the trees leaned a little funny and the cat disappeared for days. Nothing would make him come back.

Providing for Each Other

You are the one who takes it all away.
For one moment, the leaning oaks are gone, and the tall grass
where the small birds practice their incoherence.

I know but for your fingers I would lie awake
and what the barter is for their articulate flight,
the agreement we make at night,

our gutteral wail the only song for the end of the world,
before we begin blinking on again,

blinking, blinking, when the room comes back
and from the dark barn the lambs cry.

Menses

This fullness in my breasts and belly
    will ache until it goes away
breaking down like sludge running through
    the rushing gutters, this tenderness
impossible to bear, like a love
    for everything that never was. Outside
my window, even the trees look incredulous
    as if they had just remembered
their cyclical forgetting, and all week
    apart from you, the snow falls heavily
mixed with inconstant dirty rain.

I wait, and watch a single robin step
    among the paper plates that lie
face down where the fraternity boys
    have left them, smeared with ketchup
mustard, bits of soggy roll, and wonder
    how one seed erupts into a hungry
vine, spitting morning glories.
    This afternoon, I'll cook eggs
for lunch until they are white and solid
    and dead enough to eat.

What is permitted me is only a sure dull sorrow,
    and a sense of skittering on the very
edge of things, about to fall again,
    sadly deliberate as rain.
You call from the farm to tell me three
    lambs are born, black and bleating
in their stall. The ram that will not breed
    will be sold for meat, only the ewes
will be kept and nurtured and named.
    I cry for no reason and plead with you,
name them Mercy, Patience.

A Thin Smattering of Applause

Sometimes, in rain, there is an extra drumming,
and it's them

thumping their fists on the refectory tables.
Or often at night,

we hear a clicking, something like spoons,
and think it's the radiator,

but this too is a sign of their wild approval,
although who knows what really pleases them.

Now, milk
poured tinkling into the cat's tiny dish,

the hysterical barking of the neighbor's dog
in the morning, even the slurp

of mayonnaise stirred in the blue glass jar—
these are the single voices, forlorn as dirt.

But when we heave and huff together in our bed
so loud the neighbors

beat the floor with brooms
that is the real-thing deadly chorus practicing

holiday hymns, I know it.
I've seen that melody drift out the door

of your half-closed eyes, green and flickering,
and I have felt, in my own body,

the extra space their shuffling group has made
assembling.

As even now, I sputter out their
expelled breath.

The Split

I.

She'd start the fires under the bed.
I'd put them out.

She'd take the broom stick and rape all the little girls.
I'd pull them aside, stroke their cheeks, and comfort them.
—How they would cry.

Brit would fight the German soldiers.
She'd crouch by the banister waiting for them
when I was too scared.

And sometimes, she would push me farther into the back woods
        than I wanted to go.
But I was glad she did.

She was mean and she liked it.

She'd take off her clothes and dance in front of the mirror
and she'd say things and she'd swear.

She'd laugh at the crucifix, turn him upside down and watch him hang.
And she'd unhinge that piece of metal cloth between his legs
and run when she heard somebody coming
leaving me.

Mean as she was, I miss her.

Only twice have I heard her laugh since then.
Once, lying on my back in a yellow field,
I heard something that sounded like me in the back of my head
but it was Brit,

and just now, making love with you, it's hard to tell you
but I heard her laugh.

II.

It began as a fear.
There was something, not me, in the room.

And translated into a dumbfounding
forgetfulness

that stopped me on the street
puzzling

over what year it was, what month.

I began to watch my feet carefully.
Nevertheless, I suffered
accidents.

The bread knife sliced my thumb
repeatedly

the water glass shattered on the kitchen floor
and in its breaking there was a low laugh.

Looking up, I saw no one

but felt the old cat stretch inside me
feigning indifference.

Marie, I'd hear in a crowd, *Marie*
the air so thick with ghosts it was hard
breathing.

One afternoon, the trucks were humming like vacuum cleaners
in the rain.

It was impossibly lonely,
No one but me there:

I called out Brit, the city is burning,
Brit, the soldiers are coming

and she laughed so sudden and loud I turned
and saw her for one second

all insolent grace, pretending
she wasn't loving me.

What Belongs to Us

Not the memorized phone numbers.

The carefully rehearsed short cuts home.

Not the summer, shimmering like pavement, when Lucia
pushed Billy off the rabbit house and broke his arm,

or our tiny footprints in the back files.

Not the list of kings from Charlemagne to Henry

not the boxes under our beds

or Tommy's wedding day when it was so hot and Mark played the flute
and we waved at him waving from the small round window in the loft,

the great gangs of people stepping one by one into the cold water.

I have, of course, a photograph:
you and I getting up from a couch.

Full height, I stand almost two inches taller than you
but the photograph doesn't show that,
just the two of us in motion
not looking at each other, smiling.

Not even the way we said things, leaning against the kitchen counter.

Not the cabin where I burned my arm and you said, oh, you're the type
that even if it hurt, you wouldn't say.

Not even the blisters. Look.

Recovery

You have decided to live. This is your fifth
day living. Hard to sleep. Harder to eat,

the food thick on your tongue, as I watch you,
my own mouth moving.

Is this how they felt after the flood? The floor
a mess, the garden ruined,

the animals insufferable, cooped up so long?
So much work to be done.

The sodden dresses. Houses to be built.
Wood to be dried and driven and stacked. Nails!

The muddy roses. So much muck about. Hard walking.
And still a steady drizzle,

the sun like a morning moon, and all of them grumpy
and looking at each other in that new way.

We walk together, slowly, on this your fifth day
and you, occasionally, glimmer with a light

I've never seen before. It frightens me,
this new muscle in you, flexing.

I had the crutches ready. The soup simmering.
But now it is as we thought.

Can we endure it, the rain finally stopped?

Gretel, from a sudden clearing

No way back then, you remember, we decided,
but forward, deep into a wood

so darkly green, so deafening with birdsong
I stopped my ears.

And that high chime at night,
was it really the stars, or some music

running inside our heads like a dream?
I think we must have been very tired.

I think it must have been a bad broken-off
piece at the start that left us so hungry

we turned back to a path that was gone,
and lost each other, looking.

I called your name over and over again,
and still you did not come.

At night, I was afraid of the black dogs
and often I dreamed you next to me,

but even then, you were always turning
down the thick corridor of trees.

In daylight, every tree became you.
And pretending, I kissed my way through

the forest, until I stopped pretending
and stumbled, finally, here.

Here too, there are step-parents, and bread
rising, and so many other people

you may not find me at first. They speak
your name, when I speak it.

But I remember you before you became
a story. Sometimes, I feel a thorn in my foot

when there is no thorn. They tell me,
not unkindly, that I should imagine nothing here.

But I believe you are still alive.
I want to tell you about the size of the witch

and how beautiful she is. I want to tell you
the kitchen knives only look friendly,

they have a life of their own,
and that you shouldn't be sorry,

not for the bread we ate and thought
we wasted, not for turning back alone,

and that I remember how our shadows walked
always before us, and how that was a clue,

and how there are other clues
that seem like a dream but are not,

and that every day, I am less
and less afraid.

Song of the Spinster

Last night, they came again, not the dead but the living
tugging at the sleeve of my old tweed coat.

One held out a luminous clock. Another, a knife he was willing
to slit his throat with.

My mother, grunting and singing, dragged in her vacuum cleaner;
my sisters, their favorite sweaters.

Every night a jostling crowd hurries to open the kitchen door
as I stumble in with my groceries,

the eggs already broken in their carton, the milk
spilling on the linoleum like a lake I need to step over,

and every night, I turn from the chopping block
where I have set the bags down, to face them with my practiced

patient look. And all the doors lock.
Last night, a car pulled up to my curb and parked.

A man wanted only one word with me.
Behind him, my brother was chaining his bike to a parking meter

about to look up, wearing his winning smile.
My hands have never felt so ineffectual as in the night

when the dreams unreel and they crush in, plaintive, polite,
the already forgiven

and I toss like a branch in a storm of sheets, wearing my knee socks,
sleeping alone, my arms, I insist, outstretched to no one.

Keeping Still

If late at night, when watching the moon, you still
sometimes get vertigo, it's understandable
that you wish suddenly and hard for fences, for someone
to marry you. Desiring a working knowledge,
needing to know some context by heart, you might
accept anything: the room without windows,
the far and frozen North, or the prairie, the prairie
even, if it means that.

The long wide space and cold dirt that will not
be seduced into hills, and the dust, that even after
you have kicked and wept and fallen on it pounding,
will not produce a tree. It will allow you
to rise with certainty and move with the relief
of necessary things to the wash on the line,
to the small maple you brought here that must be tied
for the winter or die.

Even the prairie night, blind with snow,
when no one comes, and you no longer look
to the mirror but force your fingers to the stitching
and produce a child to help with the lambing
and the carrying of water. Although it might be years
before you turn and stop, startled
by the sweet and sudden smell of sheets snapping
in the sun, and the drunken lilac, prairie purple,
blooming by the doorway, because you planted it.

Apology

The shadows have come back, circling the room like headlights.
It is for this I leave you, sudden October, the leaves burning,
bike crash and slamming kitchen door, the boys scrambling
into the back woods.

My mother, standing at the stove, has raised her spoon, about
to ask a question, like my father, his last week living, who
wandered from room to room almost satisfied, but for something
one more thing he couldn't remember.

But all this was years ago. Last night, in a dream, my father
refused to play King Lear. He had married someone else.
She stood in the wings, wrapped in an old tweed coat, looking
at her watch. Already the facts dissemble.

Even now, as you desire me, my mother is stirring the question
into the burning soup as my father's mouth closes,
the one hundred and nine years between them walking away
like a man who has knocked on the wrong door.

The boys, crossing the street behind him, making small rude noises,
are growing out of their sneakers. My brother already wears
his nervous look. The leaves are burning. Next year, even this
will be outlawed.

Understand, I love you, even as I turn from you like this,
stumbling breathless down a dim and disappearing street behind
a man who squints at house numbers, bewildered, about to say
something I can almost hear.

Retribution

I lie in the tall grass as the sun pulls away, and the dark
pools around the trunks of the red maples and rises.

The old dog with me knows the length of her leash; still she walks
a wide circle before she settles and sleeps.

She doesn't see my father standing in the doorway, the inside light
behind him.

*

I consider that no one is home and that my father is dead.

Three hundred miles away, my brothers play slapjack at the
    kitchen table.
The attic is empty.

Long ago the girl left, her hair, by that time, the color of leaves,
but her stumbling ghost bumps, a moth at the green room door.

Her brothers are blind to this tiny light.

*

My father is moving across the grass and towards me, now past
the stacked wood, now over the small rise.

Behind him, the chickens are loose, some hole in the gate.
They are blue black in the dusk, pecking, pecking.

He is wearing his corduroys and old beaten flight jacket.
My brothers must be telling the old army story:

When he found the jap who killed his buddy, he did to him
   what he had done:
tied him to a tree, poured kerosine, lit a match.

*

Scuffling in the grass, shuffling, old whiskey breath, he is that close.

Slapjack! one shouts, leaning back in his chair.

A tractor is mounting the hill, grinding gears. The dog moans
   in her sleep.
Sister, my father is saying, *Sister, Sister.*

No one is home. *Sister*, he says. The door is swung open. The ravishing
inside light spills onto the lawn.

*

Screeching the tractor makes it. The dog looks up.
My brothers are tipping in their chairs, tipping, laughing.

They will not hear my father falling the length of the attic stairs
in the growing leaping dark.

Grosvenor Road

As teenagers, talking late at night in the family kitchen
we'd sometimes hear a scrape, a sort of gnawing

from behind, or from inside the radiator covered with wire
mesh and knotty pine, or from deep within the bottom

kitchen cupboards, where we kept the games of Monopoly
and Life with all those pieces missing. A stifled shout

or stomp would stop it. But it would start up again when
we stopped talking, impudent, incessant,

unafraid of us. No one told. At least not for some time.
That whatever-it-was blended into whatever other secrets

we never said aloud in the big expensive house, talking late
attentive to a toilet flushed that meant

our father was awake and roaming. It was years before
someone figured: rats, I don't know who exactly,

and weeks before the men could come to fix it, and then a month
or more of living through the stench of something dying,

of some things, as it turned out, and worse, when the radiator
where we tossed our soggy mittens, knocked and warmed.

Now I remember how the men left, the job done, or started,
because they couldn't get them out,

how they shook their heads and said they'd never seen anything
like it, so many.

The Beast

When I ask her what it sounds like
she says it grunts, it drools,

it's hunched over and grinning.
When I ask her who it is, she says it's her.

When I look her in the eye and ask, is it talking
to me now? Is it the beast talking when you talk?

She thinks for a minute, and says, no, it's curled up.
She's talking, but it's watching her.

Later that night, I make love for hours.
I forget my name, where my arms are, what

my tongue is doing. I think I must have cried out
unimaginable things and I think of my sister

in the next room, lying on her back, blinking in the dark.
The next morning, we make coffee and talk about the beast again.

My sister is rinsing out her cup when she turns
and says, slowly, it's *male* you know.

She looks surprised.

How Many Times

No matter how many times I try I can't stop my father
from walking into my sister's room

and I can't see any better, leaning from here to look
in his eyes. It's dark in the hall

and everyone's sleeping. This is the past
where everything is perfect already and nothing changes,

where the water glass falls to the bathroom floor
and bounces once before breaking.

Nothing. Not the small sound my sister makes, turning
over, not the thump of the dog's tail

when he opens one eye to see him stumbling back to bed
still drunk, a little bewildered.

This is exactly as I knew it would be.
And if I whisper her name, hissing a warning,

I've been doing that for years now, and still the dog
startles and growls until he sees

it's our father, and still the door opens, and she
makes that small *oh* turning over.

Letter to My Sister

We lived one life on the surface.
How could I have imagined your dark room?

I tell you I slept in the arms of the laddering beech
where even the numbing kitchen light
couldn't reach trembling in.

But this also is fiction.

I slept in fear. Then too
the beast crouched at my door
whimpering,

and it's true, I sometimes
offered you to him.

Forgive me the circumstances of my life.

This no one told us,
there is no such thing as family.

Nevertheless, today your voice reaches me,
deliberate on the wire,

and I, still older,
answer.

Perhaps this is the love we earn.

And if, with our words, the glass house cracks
and tumbles,

thus speaking, we stand clear,
the slivers sifting into our singular lives.

Isaac

When we had climbed to the top of the mountain
and there was no lamb,

I remember looking at the sky, September blue
and cold, the clouds

rushing together so fast, the ground,
for a minute, seemed to move

they rushed so quickly, I wanted to say
like horses, when

in a voice I had never heard before, he asked
me to lay myself down.

I didn't feel the rush of sudden wind,
as from a wing, that my father felt,

or hear the voice like silver he said he heard,
I didn't.

I only remember the clouds rushing across the sky
like horses

and the blood pounding inside me like water
and pushing, stumbling

down the mountain to the far pasture
to the ram that was my favorite

and weeping into its filthy matted wool,
crying out.

The Wise Men

There was nothing to tell us we were wrong,
although it had been a peculiar autumn, the ewes
refused to breed, and it was lambs
that kept my wife all winter happy.

The wood stacked, the garden packed in cellars,
there was nothing to keep us pacing the square
of light we usually protected, and the sky seemed
to lean on us, the stars to multiply.

One day we walked through town and kept on walking.
I suppose it could be expected that contentment
would dwell so long it would dull and ache,
a kind of middle-aged mistake,

but we left, and thought we wandered.
Our angry wives, they found us much the same, but
we confess we held them tight as breath inside us,
as women hold their men. We were still men

but maimed. Another kind of hurt lodged
where happiness had smouldered, another kind
of ruin, and summer came.

My Father's Oak

My father's oak, three years taller, stands taller now than I.
Two crows for company.

One gripping the telephone wire overhead, cries out.
The other, lumbering across the cold dirt like a man in a bar room,
    answers.

Blocks away, a cloud of starlings startles and lifts in one great wavering
gesture, from one anonymous tree to another,

leaves in a deliberate wind,

and I, standing here, feel for one moment, that the earth does move.

The lumbering crow stumbles and flies screeching to the wire near
    the other.

The leaves of the oak flutter, tarnished and dumb.

Speak to me, crows. Teach me to walk like a sailor.
Tell me what it is this tree superintends.

Without Devotion

Cut loose, without devotion, a man becomes a comic.
His antics are passed

around the family table and mimicked so well, years
later the family still laughs.

Without devotion, any life becomes a stranger's story
told and told again to help another sleep

or live. And it is possible
in the murmuring din of that collective loyalty

for the body to forget what it once loved.
A mouth on the mouth becomes a story mouth.

It's what they think *they* knew—what the body knew
alone, better than it ever knew anything.

Without devotion, his every gesture—
how he slouched in the family pantry, his fingers

curled into a fist, the small thing he said
while waiting for water to boil—

becomes potentially hilarious. Lucky for him
the body, sometimes, refuses translation,

that often it will speak, secretly,
in its own voice, and insist, haplessly,

on its acquired tastes. Without devotion, it might
stand among them and listen, laughing,

but look, how the body clenches,
as the much discussed smoke intermittently clears.

It has remembered the man standing, wearing
his winter coat.

Watch how it tears from the table, yapping, ferocious
in its stupid inarticulate joy.

Guests

You are at a cocktail party, talking to someone who is skewering
a small hot dog with a toothpick when you see the dead peeking
out of the pantry, motioning to you.

Your partner, looking up, just misses your raised eyebrows and
the small wave that has ended in your hand pushing through your hair.
You say, "Suddenly, I have a headache. I need a glass of water,"

and head through the pantry door where the hostess emerges carrying
          a tray
and announcing a game of charades. You allow her to pass, then step
through the empty pantry to the kitchen where the cook and three

older uncles are sitting around the kitchen table talking.
They say, "Sit down, sit down, the party's in here." You laugh,
          but decline
and go to the kitchen door where you hear something scratching
          to get in.

You open it to admit the cat that walks in precise steps to its bowl and eats.
Outside, the snow is falling like teeming arrows to the pavement
and piling up. A sudden roar of laughter comes from the living room.

Many people are calling your name. They want you on their team.
The men at the table are rising. You join them, passing by the cook
and the cat that never looks up from its dinner.

The Good Reason for Our Forgetting

Who would have the day back you saw coming in dreams
long before the actual stood like a flower

gone bad in the jar? The dreamed drunken driving,
steering from the back seat, or the garden of mazes

and he forever turning as you felt your way along
the broken bushes. Even the street of barking dogs

you finally walked through, empty-handed, pointed
to one thing. Who would have it back?

After the fact, you throw the stinking water out,
scrub the sink and turn into the new life

as if dreaming, knowing it is no dream, knowing
better. Although, some nights, you smelled it,

didn't you? A certain dissembling deep in his eyes
you could never reach, not with love

not with fearfulness. You smelled, you were almost
sure of it, something like flowers,

the beast too long neglected. But that was before,
and long before you heard the story of the boy

and his father: how, left alone for three days
they played cowboys, and how the father fell

on the first day, fell down and stayed there, playing
dead, the boy thought, and how he tried

to lift his father's head, tried to feed him
to make him stop, feed him breakfast, and how

he didn't stop, not for one minute, not once.
Who would have the day back when it happened to him?

Or the day before the day when he imagined himself
a boy, and deservedly happy?

Like the night, when the light from your lamp fell
on your face with what seemed an affectionate look.

Sorrow

So now it has our complete attention, and we are made whole.
We take it into our hands like a rope, grateful and tethered,
freed from waiting for it to happen. It is here, precisely
as we imagined.

If the man has died, if the child's illness has taken a sudden
turn, if the house has burned in the middle of night
and in winter, there is at least a kind of stopping that will
pass for peace.

Now when we speak it is with a great seriousness, and when
we touch it is with our own fingers, and when we listen
it is with our big eyes that have looked at a thing
and have not blinked.

There is no longer any reason to distrust us. When it leaves
it will leave like summer, and we will remember it as a break
in something that had seemed as unrelenting as coming rain
and we will be sorry to see it go.

Lullaby

Oh Mama, the monkeys never did come down the street.
I tried, but they never did come. There was nothing
in the back woods but woods.

The trees never moved an inch when we weren't looking.
All that thumping we heard must have been rabbits rabbits.
No angels in the bushes.

No Indians underfoot. Just the boys hanging from their
homemade houses waiting for us to come close enough
to catch.

That old beech I used to curl into never did know it.
When I carved my name there it never winced. It would
have dropped me

like an apple for someone else to bite, if it had apples.
You were right. You can tell me all you want to now.
That white sky

is only a lot of clouds moving together fast, not
an edge of paper that somebody might fold, and if
I'm having trouble with my breathing

it's that I'm still trying to make room for myself
in an envelope that's not even there. I never did
learn the birds' names, did I

but they weren't singing to me, and the lilac blooming
in the far corner of the back yard, never bloomed
I know it now, for anyone.

The Unforgiven

Luke, 23: 39-43

The reformers cackle at the gate, clutching
their carefully collected eggs and tomatoes,
a rotten harvest.

You are protected. This is as it should be.

What else have you stolen? A wife, two children,
enough to keep you living well if well beyond
your means.

Nothing anyone else wanted.

For five dollars you took the name your father
gave you. And then he died and left you
with his dusty mark.

How they quickly gathered stones.

I too took up a stone against you.
But that was centuries ago, before I cast my lot
with yours.

Today, I drop the stone in the dirt.

A traitor commits his crime but once. The rest
is retribution. Slowly, I begin to pity
even myself.

They will break your legs and insist you walk.

Endure them. Each of us suffers with envy
for the forgiven. Even I, now telling
you this.

Thank you for the gifts you sent. I needed them.

I don't care where they came from. From here,
where there is no garden, I kiss you,
on the other cheek you turn to me.

Veteran's Day

The boys of summer are climbing the building,
splayed dark against the stone, they are using ropes.
Climbing together, three of them, in T-shirts

and corduroys, hauling each other up, story
by story, stopping to speak carefully, deciding
direction: who will go first, who will belay,

who will wait on the ledge they are leaving, climbing
slowly this way, watching each other's sneakers.
Years planning, a few missteps admittedly,

several mix-ups at bus stations, a few times,
the phone ringing, no one there, but now
the boys are climbing and together, deliberate

as flies. Below them, the doors open. Grownups
stumble out, dazed from the inside dark, to watch
the boys climbing in the sun, some whistling

between their teeth, some grumbling a little.
As women, settling on the grass, spread their skirts,
the boys test their holds, put, each of them, one foot

on the ledge and bounce on their heels to feel the rope
pull taut and safe, and they don't look down. Some
of the grownups are thinking of calling the police.

The boys of summer climb, stopping now only
to rest, pressing their faces flat against the stone
to watch each other and wink, wondering

how they'll hook up to the fourth floor, where they know
there are suddenly windows. The day wanes. It is,
after all, November. The dark comes early.

Windows, as they expected, open. Hands grab
for their long American legs. The boys, laughing,
pull up their feet and stand, watching the fingers

crawl on the sill. Some of these hands they almost
recognize. Finally, there are sirens,
a kind of music. Night falls

and the boys climb in the searchlights, practicing
for the final ascent. The men directing the beams
caressing them with the incredulity

boys feel when a fly is caught finally in the fist
after a thousand times trying. The grownups
bundled into lawn chairs, drink coffee.

The boys hang like spiders and sleep, and all night
the lights caress them as the grownups watch.
At dawn, the boys of summer rise and climb again.

They are not hungry. They go slower now. There is,
between them, something invisible. Forgetting
the ropes, they stare at each story with the calculated

glances of serious climbers and they believe
everything they see. They love each other now,
climbing easily, some might say like monkeys,

they have forgotten the feel of the earth flat
underfoot, climbing like this, into autumn,
their working shoulders impossibly beautiful

as they squint, shading their eyes with sunburned fists,
the crowd, catching on, muttering story after story,
as the boys climb, by now, almost a fiction,

too high to be seen clearly. But how they glow
in their boy's strength and their beauty and their love.
What else would we have them do? They were born for this.

They know it. The crowd thickening below them
as they scramble finally to the gravelly roof
and stand, stretching then still, for one moment

before they leap, each of them, or fly, in almost
perfect swan dives, and fall
like stones, or like boys

with the thud of sure premonition to the eventual
pavement, buckling, and man-made, that has been waiting
all this time, for them, with a deep and perfect gravity.

Mary's Argument

To lead the uncommon life is not so bad.
There is an edge we come to count on
when all the normal signs don't speak,
a startled vigilance that keeps us waking
to watch the moon, the peculiar stars;
the usual, underfoot, no more a solid comfort
than a rock that might move as a turtle moves,
so slowly only the nervous feel the sudden bump
of the familiar giving way to unrequested astonishment.
And for a small time, the sheer cliff of everything
we never knew can rise in front of us
like the warm dark, where starlight
has its constant conception, where the *idea* of turtle
blinked and was: a wry joke, an intricate affection.

Encounter

First, the little cuts, then the bigger ones,
the biggest, the burns. This is what God did
when he wanted to love you.

She didn't expect to meet him on the stairway
no one used but she did, because she was
afraid of the elevator, the locked room.

She didn't expect him to look like that, to be
so patient, first the little ones, then
the big ones. Everything

in due time, he said, I've got all the time
in the world. She didn't imagine it would take
so long, the breaking.

He did it three times before he did it. Love?
She had imagined it differently, something
coming home to her,

an end to waiting. And she did stop, when
the big cuts came. It was all there was,
the burning, and that's what God was

everywhere at once. Someone had already
told her that, only not in his voice. He was
inside her now—

the bigger ones, then the burning—and gone,
then back again. This was eternity, when
nothing happened that wasn't

already happening. She couldn't remember.
After the burning, even the light went quiet.
She didn't think God would be so

specific, so delicate—inside her elbow, under
her arm, the back of her neck
and her knees.

It's true, she struggled at first, until after
the breaking. Then God was with her, and she
was with him.

The National Poetry Series 1987

The Good Thief
Marie Howe
Selected by Margaret Atwood/Persea Books

The Singing Underneath
Jeffrey Harrison
Selected by James Merrill/E. P. Dutton

The Hand of God and a Few Bright Flowers
William Olsen
Selected by David Wagoner/University of Illinois Press

A Guide to Forgetting
Jeffrey Skinner
Selected by Tess Gallagher/Graywolf Press

New Math
Leigh Cole Swenson
Selected by Michael Palmer/William Morrow & Company

The National Poetry Series was established in 1978 to publish five collections of poetry annually through five participating publishers. The manuscripts are selected by five poets of national reputation. Publication is funded by the Copernicus Society of America, James A. Michener, Edward J. Piszek, The National Endowment for the Arts, the Friends of the National Poetry Series, and the five publishers—E. P. Dutton, Graywolf Press, William Morrow & Co., Persea Books, and the University of Illinois Press.